Concert and Contest COLLECTION

Compiled and Edited by H. VOXMAN

for

OBOE with piano accompaniment

CONTENTS

RUBANK®

HAL•LEONARD® CORPORATION

7777 W. BLUEMOUND RD. P.O. BOX 13819 MILWAUKEE, WI 53213

Ariette
from Panurge

A. E. M. GRÉTRY
Transcribed by H. Voxman

Aria and Rondinella

G. F. HANDEL
Transcribed by H. Voxman

Two Menuettos
from Flute Sonata in C

I

J. S. BACH
Transcribed by H. Voxman

II

Menuetto I da capo

Gavotta

A. GOEDICKE, Op. 80, No. 1
Transcribed by H. Voxman

Menuetto and Presto
from Trio V

F. J. HAYDN
Transcribed by H. Voxman

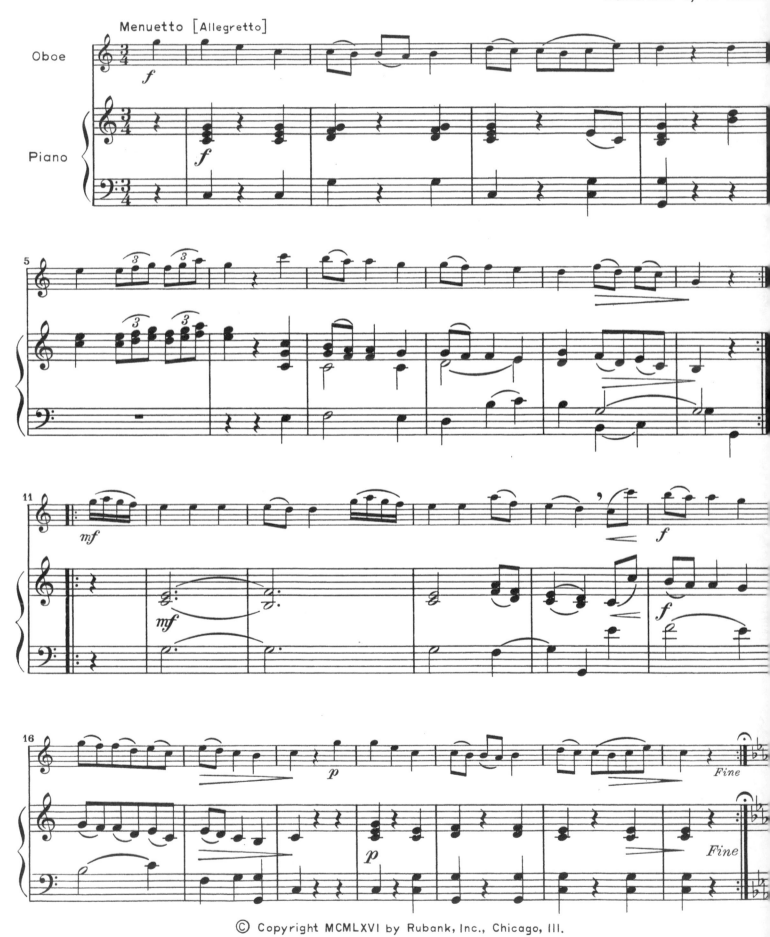

TRIO

Menuetto D. C. al Fine

Presto D. C. al Fine
(with repeats)

Romance

R. SCHUMANN, Op. 94, No. 1
Edited by H. Voxman

Sinfonia

(Arioso)
from Cantata No. 156*

J. S. BACH
Transcribed by H. Voxman

* This Cantata was composed by Bach ca. 1730. The original scoring of the Sinfonia is for solo oboe, strings, and continuo. The eighth-note accompaniment figures (treble) should probably be played quasi pizzicato. Bach also used this melody in a more elaborate version in his F minor Concerto for clavier.

Mélodie

CLÉMENT LENOM
Edited by H. Voxman

Andante and Allegro
from Sonata in G Major

J. B. LOEILLET
Arr. by A. Béon

Edited by H. Voxman

28

Pièce in G Minor

GABRIEL PIERNÉ, Op. 5
Edited by H. Voxman

33

Adagio and Allegro

LEROY OSTRANSKY

Sonata No. 1

G. F. HANDEL
Edited by H. Voxman

Begin all trills in the Sonata on the upper note.

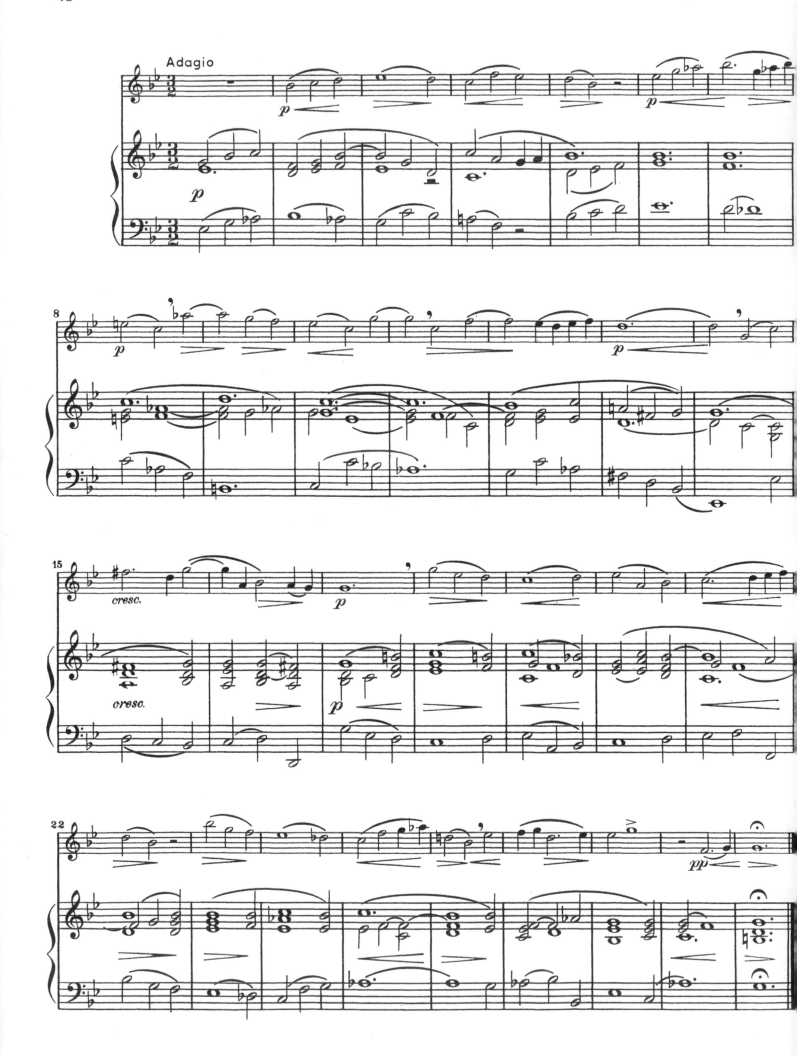

Sonatina
Based on Divertimento No. 2

W. A. MOZART
Transcribed by H. Voxman

52

TRIO

Menuetto da capo al Fine

Allegro Moderato
from Trio No. 1 (London)

F. J. HAYDN
Adapted by R. Hervig

Colloquy

IRA P. SCHWARZ

Rubank Oboe Solos

WITH PIANO ACCOMPANIMENT

RUBANK®

HAL•LEONARD® CORPORATION

7777 W. BLUEMOUND RD. P.O. BOX 13819 MILWAUKEE, WI 53213